W9-AAU-833

Nighty Night, Baby Jesus

A Noisy Nativity

By

Molly Schaar Idle

Abingdon Press

Nashville

Nighty Night, Baby Jesus

Original Editon ISBN: 978-1-426-70030-9
Copyright © 2009 by Molly Schaar Idle
All Rights Reserved.

Nighty Night, Baby Jesus / Nighty Night, Noah
Copyright © 2012 by Molly Schaar Idle
All Rights Reserved.

No part of this work may be reproduced or transmitted in any form or by any means, electronic or mechanical, including photocopying and recording, or by any information storage or retrieval system, except as may be expressly permitted by the 1976 Copyright Act or by permission in writing from the publisher. Requests for permission should be submitted in writing to: Rights and Permission, Abingdon Press, 201 Eighth Avenue, South, P.O. Box 801, Nashville, TN 37202-0801; faxed to (615) 749-6128; or sent via e-mail to *permissions@abingdonpress.com*.

978-1-426-75638-2
PACP01125392-01

12 13 14 15 16 17 18 19 20 21 —10 9 8 7 6 5 4 3 2 1

Printed in China

For Steve

and

our baby boys from heaven

One night in sleepy Bethlehem
a single star shone down,
illuminating miracles
below in that small town.

Outside the silent stable
all was dark that holy night.
But, rising from the manger
came the Son's warm, glowing light.

So bright it woke the Rooster,
who thought day had come anew.
He crowed to wake the animals with

"COCK-A-DOODLE-DO!"

Up for work, the Ox plowed toward
his breakfast in the manger.
But, in place of food, he found
a perfect Little Stranger.

The Ox was taken by surprise
and sounded a low

"MOO."

This roused the Cow and her small Calf,
who sounded their 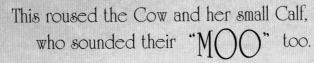 "MOO" too.

On wobbly legs, the Calf set out
to find some hay to graze.
Then face to face and nose to nose,
she met the Baby's gaze.

This struck the Donkey funny,
and he laughed at what he saw—

threw back his head, kicked up his heels,
and burst out with "HEE-AW!"

The Camel, taking in the scene,
　　watched as the Donkey brayed.
Then, wisely, knelt before the crib,
　　and *silently* she prayed.

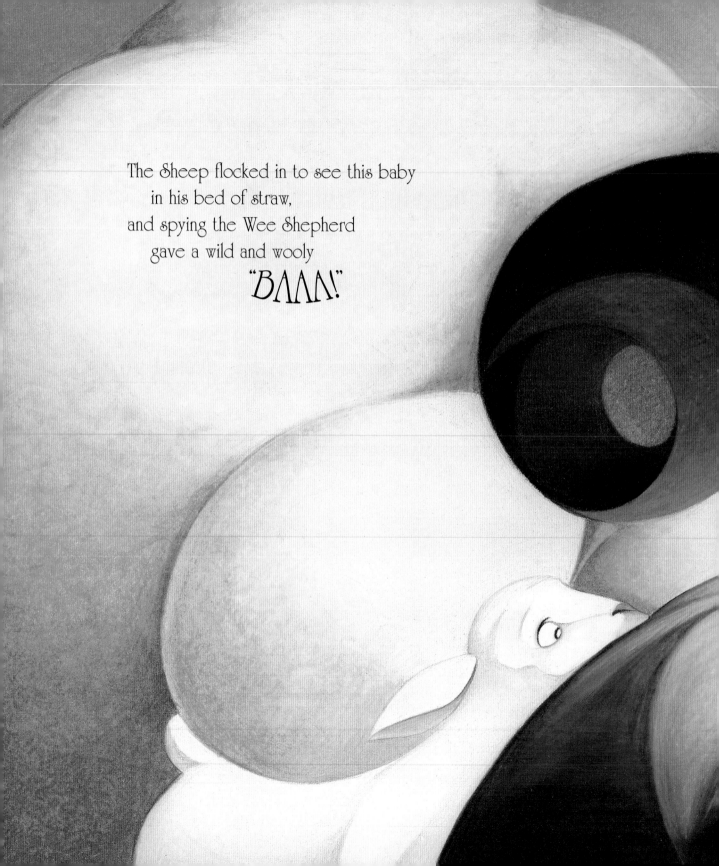

The Sheep flocked in to see this baby
in his bed of straw,
and spying the Wee Shepherd
gave a wild and wooly

"BAAA!"

The Goat heard all the ruckus
and came in to have his say.
His mouth was full as usual,
but he "MAΛΛeδ" anyway.

And then, the Hen with Chicks in tow,
　　came in to take a peep.
All standing up on tiny toes,
　　they chorused

　　　CHEEP! CHEEP! CHEEP!

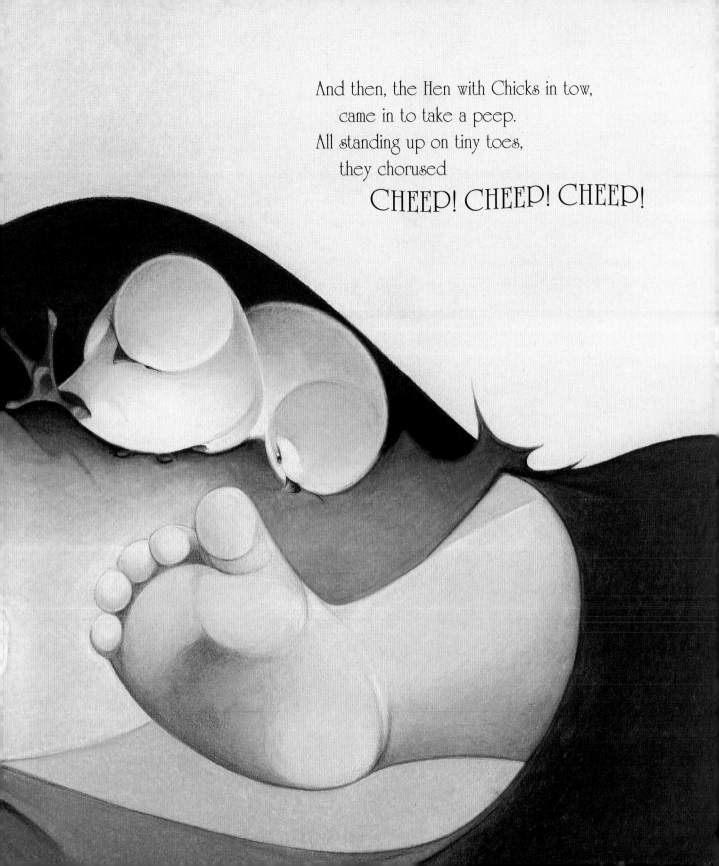

The Dog came in and joined the rest,
he wagged from end to end.
This Little Boy in swaddling clothes
was sure to be a friend.

He chased the chickens round about
and barked a joyous "WOOF!"

And it was this that woke the Cat
   so lazily aloof.

      She yawned and stretched, and unimpressed,
         prepared to bathe her fur.
      But then a tiny hand, so soft,
      reached up and made her

          "PURRRRRRRR."

From "COCK-A-DOODLE-DO"
to "PURRRRRRRR,"
each made a joyful sound.
Until, with Mary's gentle "Shhh . . ."
a hush fell all around.

His mother picked him up
and cooed a gentle lullaby.
Her Baby Boy from heaven yawned
and closed his sleepy eyes.

"Sweet dreams," she whispered softly,
precious bundle in her lap.
Time for her Son to settle down
and have a little nap.

Nighty night, sweet Baby Jesus,
   all is calm, all is bright,
while up above the star shines down—
   your heavenly night-light.

Nighty Night, Baby Jesus.

"Now I lay me down to sleep,
I pray the Lord my soul to keep . . ."

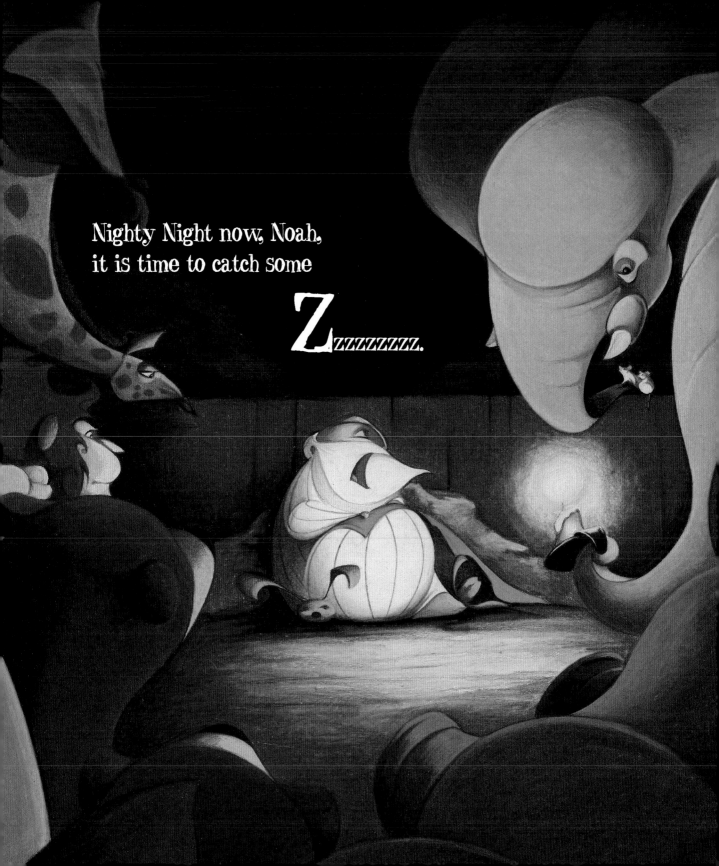

Nighty Night now, Noah,
it is time to catch some

ZZZZZZZZZ.

Quails' sleepy heads bob up and down —
each with a plume adorned.

Rhinoceros wear sleeping caps
upon their heads and horns.

Sheep count themselves to fall asleep
as they lie in the moonlight.

Tortoises, tucked in their shells,
can be sure they will sleep tight.

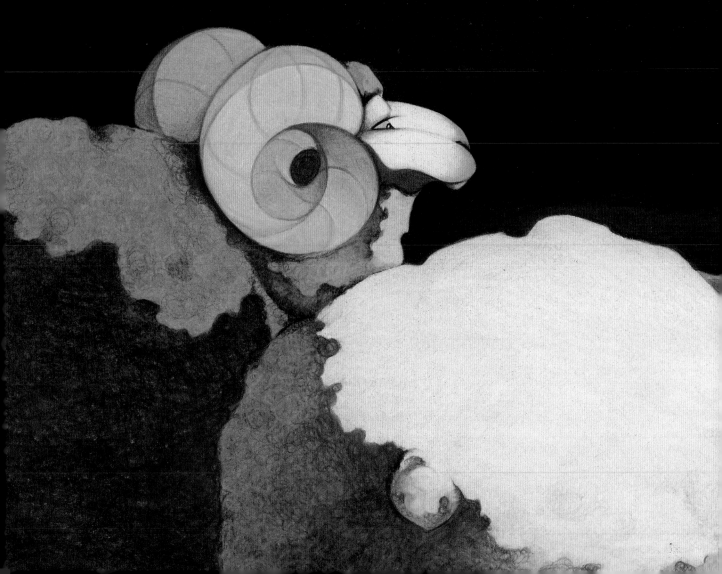

Underwater —
animals are snoozing in the deep.

Violet Fish and Whales
'neath the waves are fast asleep.

X - Ray Fish —
like nightlights —
can illuminate the dark
For all the creatures in the ocean
underneath the ark.

Yaks stop yakking and start yawning —
rocked to sleep upon the seas.

O

Ostriches and **P**ossums

are the oddest sleepers found.

One pair dozes upside down —
the other underground!

Night owls are nocturnal. They won't sleep a single wink.

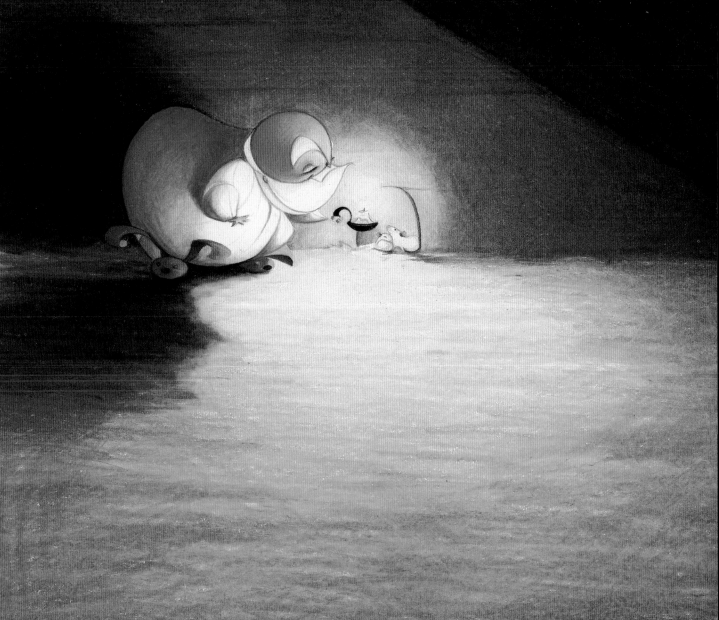

Mice are barely stirring as the ark rocks in the drink.

Lions roar in protest —
"One more story must be read!"

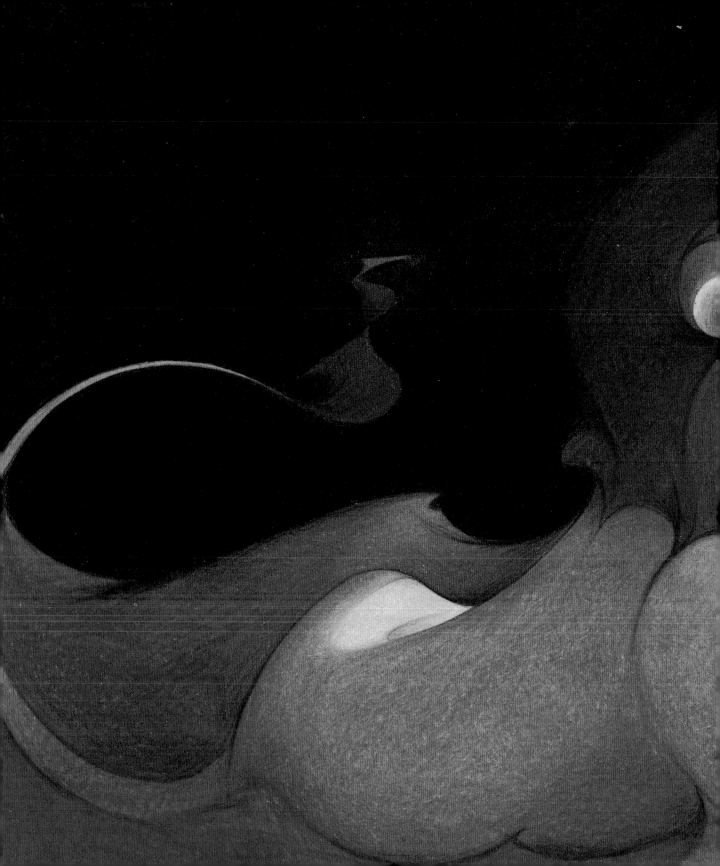

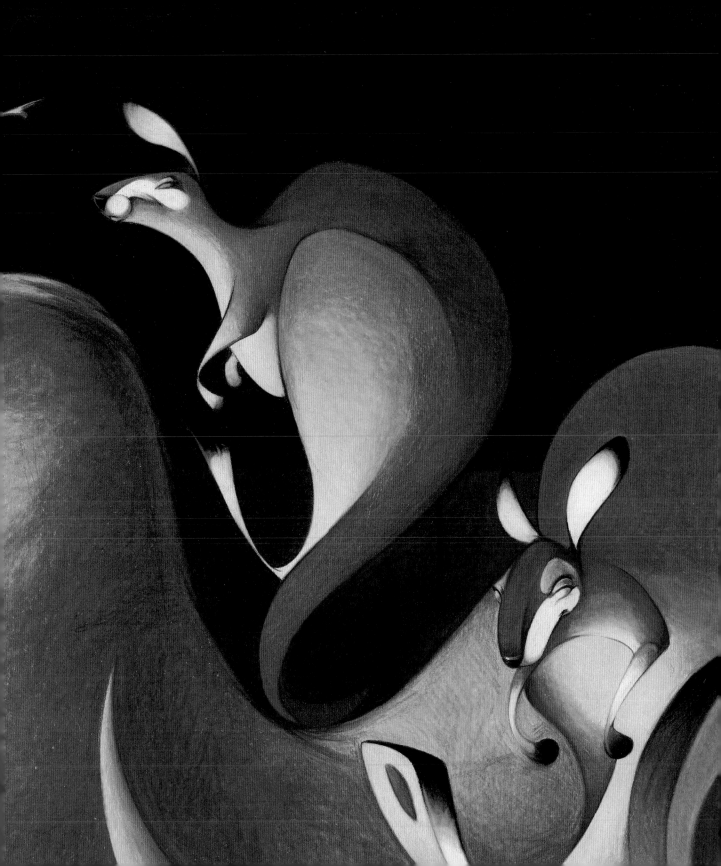

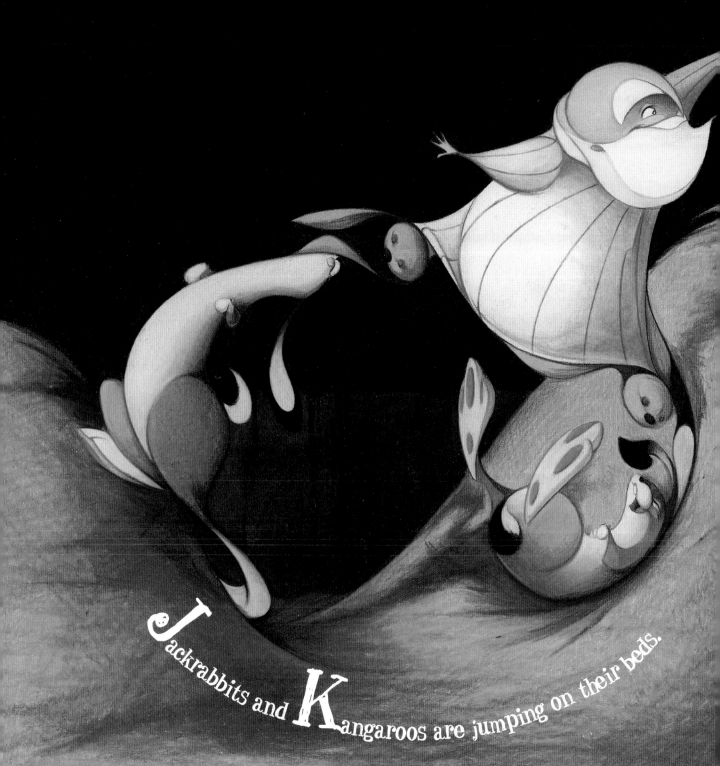

Jackrabbits and **K**angaroos are jumping on their beds.

Hippopotami are heavy sleepers when they hit the sack!

Ibises, their earmuffed neighbors, are insomniacs.

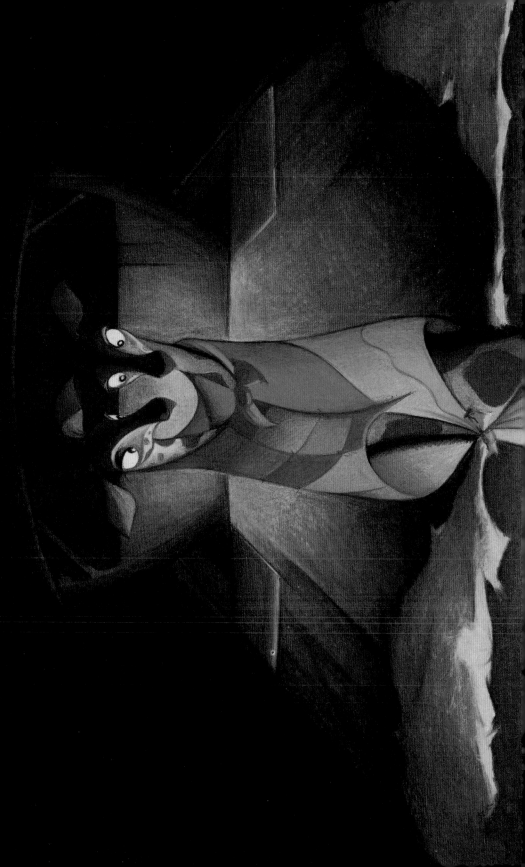

Flamingos and Giraffes

need extra blankets for, you see,

One needs covers for their necks — the other for their knees!

Elephants remember
to say "thank you" in their prayers
For friends and food — like peanuts...
All the blessings that are theirs.

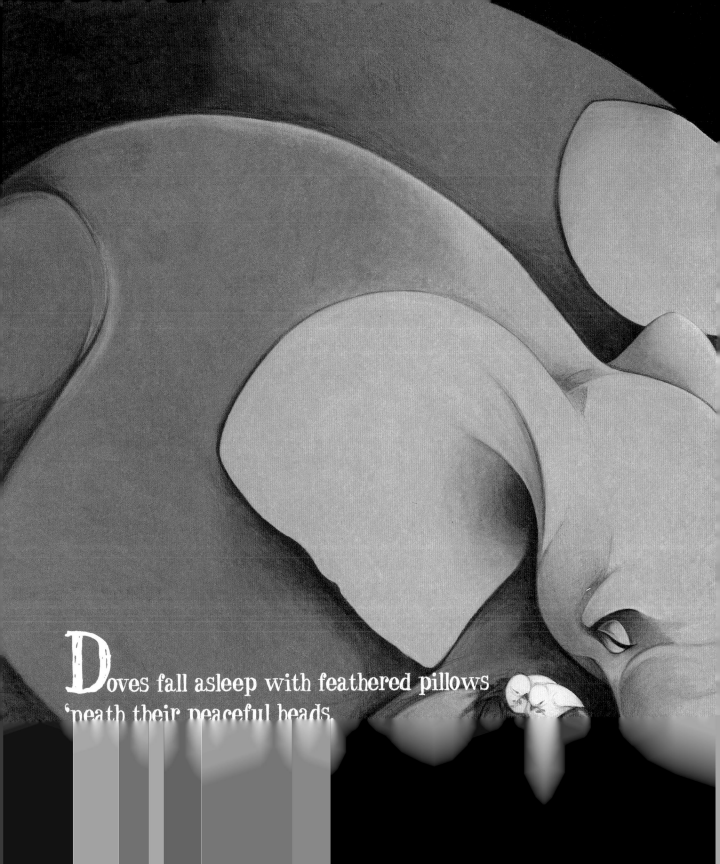

Doves fall asleep with feathered pillows
'neath their peaceful heads.

*C*amels need *another* drink   before they go to bed . . .

Bears each need a big bear hug
to see them through the night.

Alligators brush their teeth
till each is pearly white.

For 40 Days and 40 Nights rain fell upon the ark,
Now all aboard catch 40 winks as daylight turns to dark.

Noah tucks them, two by two, into their beds with care
To see that each from A to Z will sleep in cozy pairs.

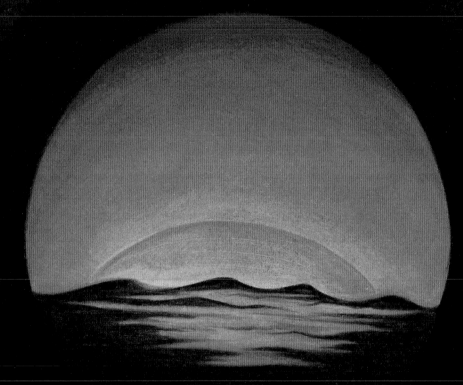

To my Two
John and Tom

Nighty Night, Noah

An Ark Alphabet
by
Molly Schaar Idle

Abingdon Press

Nashville

NIGHTY NIGHT, NOAH

Original Edition ISBN: 978-0-687-64691-3
Copyright © 2008 by Molly Schaar Idle
All Rights Reserved.

Nighty Night, Baby Jesus / Nighty Night, Noah
Copyright © 2012 by Molly Schaar Idle
All Rights Reserved.

No part of this work may be reproduced or transmitted in any form or by any means,
electronic or mechanical, including photocopying and recording, or by any information storage
or retrieval system, except as may be expressly permitted by the 1976 Copyright Act
or by permission in writing from the publisher.
Requests for permission should be submitted in writing to:
Rights and Permissions, The United Methodist Publishing House, 201 Eighth Avenue, South,
P.O. Box 801, Nashville, TN 37202-0801; faxed to (615) 749-6128;
or sent via e-mail to *permissions@abingdonpress.com*.

978-1-426-75638-2

PACP01125392-01

12 13 14 15 16 17 18 19 20 21—10 9 8 7 6 5 4 3 2 1

Printed in China